I0420946

How to Raise Backyard Honey Bees:

The Complete Guide to Beekeeping from Setting up Your Hive to Collecting Honey

Introduction

I want to thank you and congratulate you for buying the book, *"How to Raise Backyard Honey Bees."*

Beekeeping has been a favorite activity of mankind over the centuries. Backyard beekeeping in particular has gained a lot of traction due the many benefits derived from it. The major reason you probably want to have some backyard bees is the honey. Yes, honey is a very healthy natural sweetener and preservative. However, this is only one of the many reasons you might be interested in this hobby. Pollination of your garden is something the bees will happily do thus ensuring a bountiful harvest. Bees provide other products too such as beeswax, royal jelly, pollen and propolis which can be very useful to your homestead or they can even earn you a good source of revenue.

In this book, we shall look at how you can become a successful backyard beekeeper and effectively manage your bees to obtain honey.

Disclaimer

The information herein is geared towards giving definite and dependable data concerning the theme and issue covered. The distribution is sold with the understanding that the distributor, writer or publisher is not qualified or otherwise to give medical, legal or financial advice. In the event that guidance is needed, a legitimate or proficient person in the profession ought to be sought.

It is unlawful to repeat, copy, or retransmit any piece of this document by either electronic means or in printed configuration. Redistribution of this production in any capacity is not permitted unless the distributor has explicit consent from the author or publisher. All rights held.

The information herein is understood to be truthful. In that any risk, regarding use or misuse, of any approaches, techniques, or direction contained inside is the lone and utter responsibility of the reader. By no means will any legitimate or illegitimate obligation or fault be held against the distributor, publisher, author or other, for any reparation, harms, or money related misfortune because of the data herein, either straightforward or by implication.

Particular creators possess all copyrights not held by the distributor.

The data thus is offered for information purposes only. The presentation of the data is without contract or any kind of insurance certification.

The trademarks that are utilized are without any consent or support by the trademark owner. All trademarks and brands inside this book are for clarifying purposes only and are owned by the owners themselves, not affiliated with this document.

Cover Photo CC0 Public Domain pixabay.com
CopyScape Verified October 27, 2015
Edited December 9, 2015

Contents

Chapter 1: Why Keep Bees

There are many benefits why you should have some backyard hives. Let's look at them in greater detail. It might just act as extra motivation to you to engage in this sweet and rewarding activity.

Sharing the hobby with friends

One of the most enjoyable things as a beekeeper will be explaining and sharing your hobby with eager friends trying to learn how you do it. This is a very nice experience as you get to encourage other people to get into this activity as well. There have been reports of decreased bee colonies all over the world. Due to factors such as chemical pesticides, disease, pests and climate change, bees are becoming fewer and fewer. Among the dangers of this is that gardens and farms are suffering from low production due to reduced pollination. Playing your part in reversing this trend by keeping bees and encouraging your friends to do so as well is quite rewarding. Bees are exciting creatures which you'll learn a lot from. Their highly structured social nature makes them a good sport. You can never learn enough about bees. Each day you learn something new. You'll then pass this education on to anybody who'll require it. There also something magical about working with bees. When you are working with bees, you feel connected to nature and this act as a stress reliever. It can be called the bee therapy which only those who have worked with bees can attest to.

Harvesting your own honey

This is by far the biggest motivator to having some backyard bees. There's nothing as delicious as your own home produced honey. The possibility of harvesting over 100 pounds of honey is very enticing as this will be more than enough for your home. You could even share or sell the surplus.

Honey is one of the natural products with numerous health benefits. It has been used by generations as a health product, food, natural sweetener, and as a preservative. Honey has particularly been used to treat people with allergies. The fact that bees make honey from pollen collected from different flowers makes it a versatile product. If you are allergic to pollen, this might come in handy as the pollen present in honey will immunize your body. That's not all; honey has been proven to have anti-microbial properties thus used to treat wounds and burns. It's also used in skin and hair products. Such is the versatility of honey that you shouldn't afford not having any at home. The good thing with backyard produced honey is that you are 100% sure of its quality unlike the ones you buy in stores.

CC0 Public Domain pixabay.com

Bees are eager pollinators.

If you have a garden where you have flowers, fruits or vegetables, you'll notice a big increase in productivity of these once you keep some bees close. This is because bees are eager pollinators. They move from flower to flower searching for pollen which they use to make honey. In the course of doing so, they fertilize your plants thus ensuring higher production. This, even more than producing honey, is the most important role bees play in nature. Bees are responsible for around 80% of the pollination. In light of our earlier observation that bee colonies have drastically reduced, there is the real threat facing farmers of reduced production. You might wonder how the backyard bees will help in this, as we'll be finding out in later chapters, bees move for miles in search of pollen. So by keeping backyard bees, you'll be helping the ecosystem remain sustainable in your own small way. Your one hive can make such a big difference.

Chapter 2: Tools and Equipment You Need

There are a few essential tools and equipment you'll need in your beekeeping journey. It will actually be good for you to assemble these tools and equipment even before you bring in the bees. I will take you through the essential equipment you'll need, others will be assembled along the way as need arises.

CC0 Public Domain pixabay.com

Beekeepers veil

This is the very first thing you need to have before you bring in the bees. Never visit your beehive without a veil. Most bees are gentle and will pose no threat to you, but before you can fully interact and understand your bee colony, always open the beehive with a veil. There are cases of Africanized bee colonies which are known to be aggressive. However, this shouldn't be much concern. Many bee colonies are gentle and will not attack, however, they are super curious and will explore anything new that comes to them. Imagine them exploring your face, nose, ears, or even getting inside your clothing. Veils will come in different shapes, sizes and prices. At first, I would advise you to go for a basic veil which is not so expensive but will cover you adequately. If you live in a location known for aggressive bees, then go for a full body suit which will offer maximum protection. If you have any family member or friend who might also be interested in this hobby, get an extra veil to keep them safe too as they interact with the bees.

Gloves

You might need gloves at specific times in the beekeeping season. However, use of gloves is not necessary at all times as it can inhibit your sense of touch leading to injuries or death to your bees. The only times you'll require a glove will be when harvesting honey or late in the season when the colony is large and strong. During these two times, even gentle bees might be aggressive since they want to protect their honey. Get yourself a good pair of gloves.

Smoker

This is absolutely essential to a beekeeper. Smoke calms bees and allows you to work on a hive or inspect the colony for anything unusual. You'll need a smoker when harvesting the honey. Bees are very protective of the honey as this is their stored food. A smoker is designed to bellow smoke into the direction of the hive. Smoke calms the bees by masking the pheromones that are released by the guard bees in case of a threat. Without the pheromone, the bees won't attack. Smoke will also make the bees eat honey to fill up their stomachs in anticipation of a possible evacuation. Filled up bees don't attack. The smoker is a simple device, just a chamber for burning up the material used to produce the smoke and a bellow directing the smoke. You can actually make a smoker yourself from home.

Hive tool

This is a like a mini crow bar which you'll use to loosen hive parts, scrape wax, manipulate frames and open up the hive. It's just a simple tool that will make your work easier.

Bee brush

You'll use it wipe bees from the frames and also from your clothing. Bees will tend to swarm around you and frames as you open up the hive. This brush will gently wipe them off from any surface without injuring them. You could also use a goose feather to do the same.

Chapter 3: Overcoming the Fear of Getting Stung

Many people would like to get to beekeeping but the fear of getting stung holds them back. In fact bees are known for stinging as equally as they are known for their honey. Now keeping them in the backyard becomes a real worry not only for you, but your family and neighbors. However, most bees are usually very calm and docile. If you purchase your colony from experienced honey bee breeders, you'll not have to fear getting stung. You should reassure your family and neighbors of this as well even as you highlight all the benefits that having these bees will have. You can even promise your neighbor some honey after your first harvest.

If you follow the necessary precaution when handling bees, you'll get through a whole season without even a single sting. One thing I'll advise you this early is that you should always take your time when approaching a hive, and handling bees, never rush as bees are likely to interpret this as a threat. Give them enough time to register your presence and get used to you. In addition, before you understand your bee colony, always wear a veil and use a smoker when doing anything at the hive. Approach the hive during favorable weather, this is usually midday. At this time many bees are out there in the fields collecting nectar. When handling the frames full of bees, make sure you grip it firmly; you do not want to drop it. Any sudden movement is a threat to the bees and they will react aggressively. On this point do not swat on them even if they get into contact with your bare skin. They will be just exploring and will rarely sting. If plan to attend to the hive, make sure you do not have any body odor. Take a bath and do not apply any perfume.

However, even after you observe all these, you'll get the occasional sting. This is expected of any beekeeper. The first thing you'll have to do is to remove the stinger. It's usually visible and you can just pinch it off your skin or rub the area till it detaches. Then, you should smoke the stung area to mask the pheromone scent left behind by the bee. This scent usually raises an alarm and you are likely to be stung by more bees. Compress the area with cold clothing to alleviate the discomfort. You should also apply antihistamine especially if you are prone to swelling. A paste made from baking soda will also work with some people. In a small percentage of the population, bee stings trigger severe allergic reactions. Most people will experience some redness, itching and a little pain which will disappear in a few minutes. These are not considered allergic reactions. The allergic reactions will involve serious symptoms like swelling beyond the area of the sting, shortness of breath and even loss of consciousness. Death has been reported as well. However, this is a small percentage of the population. If you are worried of such a scenario and you live a considerable distance from a medical facility, you could purchase an emergency sting kit prescribed by a doctor. This will have a dosage of epinephrine which you can inject to the allergic person.

Some beekeepers actually make a few bees actually sting them early in the season so that they could build some form of resistance. This sounds weird but they claim it works. I don't think a beginner would be comfortable with such an idea!

Chapter 4: Setting Up Your Hive

The hive is the single most important item you'll require. You'll need to get this right to ensure success in your beekeeping journey. The hive is where the bee colony will call home. Apart from collecting nectar, everything else the bees do will be inside the hive. It's thus important to provide them a functional structure. The fact that this hive will be located in your backyard will also pose some unique challenges. You need to carefully to consider where to place it. You will also need to consider the design and any decoration you might add to your hive to make it attractive and fit in the general character of you backyard. You'll also need a hive that will make it easy for you to carry out inspections, harvest honey and manage the colony conveniently to both yourself and the bees. You'll have the option of either buying a hive or building one. This will depend on your expertise in building. If you have the tools necessary and you could easily find the materials to build a hive, then you could always look for a design of the different hives and choose the best one. I would suggest purchasing your first hive so as to acquaint yourself with the parts and workings of a hive.

The basic parts of a hive

Let's look at the basic parts of a hive and their work to have a deeper understanding of the beehive. The bee colony is highly structured with the different bees having different functions. They need a hive that facilitates this for maximum production of honey.

Hive stand

A hive stand will be needed depending on where you choose to place your hive. You can't place the hive on the ground due to wet ground, air circulation, predators (bees too have them) and obstruction by ground plants. It will also be strenuous to you working on a hive that is completely on the ground. The hive stand comes in handy as you won't have to think about raising or suspending you hive.

Bottom board

The bottom board can be called the floor of the beehive. It protects your bees from wet ground. It will consist if a sold piece of wood, surrounded by several rails. You could choose to use the screened bottom board to improve ventilation.

Entrance reducer

A notched wooden piece will serve as an entrance reducer. It fits between the bottom board and the first deep super. Its main purpose is to control ventilation and temperature in the winter month. It also serves to limit bee access to the hive when the colony is new. The entrance reducer should be easily detachable from the hive. You can adjust, remove or reintroduce it as necessary.

Slatted rack

This is not very necessary to the hive. It's used to offer ventilation and reduce hive congestion. If you live in a place where summers are really hot, then you should consider it. It provides more space between the entrance and the brood chamber. This space ensures the bees are able to get in more air to the hive. The queen will be able to lay more eggs all the way down the frame.

Deep super and frames

These are the heart of the hive. It's where the bees will build their wax into and have the brood chamber. The frames may be made from wood or plastic or even a combination of the two. The bees will store honey for their young ones and for their own use here. You should never harvest honey from here. Depending on the size of you hive, you'll have a different number of frames.

Queen excluder

This is a rack with holes in it its used to allow worker bees get through but excludes the queen bee. The queen is bigger than any other bee in the colony.

This exclusion is meant to prevent the queen from laying eggs in the honey super. You could also use the queen excluder to have two queens in the same hive

Honey super and frames

This is the all-important part for the bee keeper. It is the box that holds the frames where the bees store their honey. The frames come in different sizes, medium shallow and deep. For backyard bees, use the medium or shallow since these supers will be very heavy when filled with honey. When starting out, you could have just one honey super but in the second and subsequent seasons, you might add more depending on how much honey your colony produces . You can stack as many honey supers as possible.

Inner and outer covers

The inner covers will appear like a shallow tray. It will have ventilation hole in the center. The tray side of the inner cover should face up. The outer cover should be a sturdy waterproof material that protects the bees from the elements.

Identifying the Ideal Location for your Hive.

Where should you keep your hive? Bees are sensitive creatures and for them to perform optimally, you should try to make them comfortable. However, you should also note bees are versatile creatures able to quickly adapt to different conditions. That's why they survive in the wild, in cities, in backyards, in rooftops and even in people's houses. There a few guidelines you need to follow to try making them comfortable. Since you are having them in your backyard, I'll concentrate on what you do and where to identify the best spot for them.

Easy access

The first thing you want is to make the ease to the hives to be easy for the bees and for you. For the bees, place the hive in such a manner that the entrance will not have anything close blocking it, make the flight path to the entrance as direct as possible. The bees will be foraging for nectar for miles and the last thing you want is for them to struggle getting to the hive. For your own case, you'll need to conduct inspections on your hive frequently, you might also need to show people around your hive, so place the hive where you'll be able to access and work on it without too much of a hassle. Honey will also have some considerable weight, even though I know you are thinking that this can't be a problem, you want a bountiful harvest, but place the hive where you'll easily carry your honey back to the house

Wind and drainage

It goes without saying that the hive should be in a well-drained place. Normally, you'll place the hive in a hive stand but even then, make sure no water should get into the hive; otherwise your colony may get uncomfortable and leave. Also avoid a location where wind blows directly into the hive. You might reduce this by planting some trees to block the winds and even more importantly regulate the flight path of the bees. In the backyard, the hive may be close to your neighbor's property and the spirit for good neighborliness, don't let the bees become a bother. Plant trees behind your hive to regulate the flight path and probably even block sight of the hive to avoid disputes. If trees are not an option, you may choose to erect a fence. A live fence would be a better idea.

Sunlight

The ideal location should be your hive facing to the south east. This is to ensure your bees are up early in the morning and they can start their main duty which is to forage for pollen. The hive should however not only the sun's rays to beam through. Normally most hives will be designed in such a manner that this won't happen. Aim for dappled sunlight to the hive. Do not place the hive in a deep shade as this might make the hive damp.

Ventilation

This is very important; bees need lots of fresh air. They work hard to regulate the temperatures inside the hive. There's a lot going on inside. The queen lays eggs, there are other eggs hatching and others growing into bees, other bees are busy working the pollen to make honey, yet other bees are working hard to guard the hive against any threat. All these activities will need some good ventilation. By design, hives will ensure enough air flows through them. However, you should also try to ensure you place the hive in a place where air flows easily. You shouldn't for instance place the hive in a gulley.

Level firm ground

The hive should be level from side to side. This is important to the bees. You could taper it about an inch to the front to ensure water drains out of the hive. The ground you choose should be firm. Bees don't like their home being shaky. This can irritate them to the point of finding a new home. You could build a platform for them to ensure this. The areas around the hive should be free of long grasses. They might block the entrance to the hive. To avoid working on this a lot of times, mulch the area to prevent the grass from growing.

It's understandable if you aren't able to math all these conditions. You should however try to make the bees as comfortable as possible based on the circumstances. Comfortable bees are happy bees and happy bees produce more honey. If you ever need to move the hive, you will have to be very careful. Once colony established, it becomes difficult for your bees to move to a different location even if it's a few yards within your backyard. Bees normally develop their flight paths depending on different landmarks around their hive. Moving the hive totally disorients them. if you have to move the hive, try doing so a few yards at a time. Allow them to adjust then move a few yards again till you get to the new location.

Dressing up your hive

This is important for backyard hives. You don't want an ugly structure to just come up in your background and seem out of character. You want to maintain some beauty and functionality to your hive. A well looking hive that fits into your backyard will be an attraction to your visitors. Your neighbors are also less likely to complain if the hive is beautiful. However in most of the alterations I suggest here to your hive, always try to think them through in regards to your specific hive and location setting. Do not favor design over safety.

Painting your hive

This can turn out to be very interesting. You can decide to paint your hive anything you want. Any color will also be good, though bees love brighter colors. (Note this even when approaching them with your clothing). Paint you beehive to fit into the character of your home, you could paint in the same color as your house, you could do whimsical, abstract designs really, there are no rules. Just do your thing but be very creative.

Using exotic wood for your hive

How cute can this turn out to be. Just imagine a hive made from long lasting exotic wood. It might be very expensive and impractical to the commercial bee farmer but to a backyard bee keeper, it might be something to explore. If you make the hive yourself, assemble the exotic woods and build the hive. If you purchase the hive, you could try shopping around to find such a hive or you could walk to a bee store and explain to them what you need. They will gladly provide one for you.

Using decorative handles and embellishments

You can choose to have some unique handles and add any embellishment you can to your hive just to spruce things up. However, in the handles make sure that they are capable of lifting the hive. Hives with a bee colony can get very heavy even past 90 pounds. As with the embellishments, make sure it doesn't interfere with any working part of the hive. You could choose an antique look for your hive.

Alternative roof

You could choose to have a different roof design than the ones with common bee hives. A peaked roof is more attractive than a flat roof. You could also choose different materials such as copper which are more attractive.

Lastly you could decide to install a webcam to your hive. Yeah, the hive is not left behind the technological advancements of our time. You will use the webcam to monitor and observe your bees remotely. You might be far away from home for days but you need to see things around. This will come in handy.

Chapter 5: Identifying the Three Different Castes of Bees

As you might know, we have three different castes of bees in a hive we have the queen, worker and drone bees. Each of these bees has a distinct role to play in the life of the colony. Bees are highly organized and efficient in their operations and understanding these castes will make you a better beekeeper.

CC0 Public Domain pixabay.com

The Queen Bee

She is the most important bee in the colony she gives life to new bees and controls what happens in the colony and other bees look after her like the queen she is. Without a queen, the colony can't survive. At any given time, there's only one queen, though there are some modern hive designs with a queen excluder which can accommodate two queens. However, this is more advanced bee keeping.

It's easy to identify the queen bee as she is the largest bee in the colony. She has a long body. The queen primary function is to lay eggs which then hatch to new bees. This ensures continuity is the colony. The queen can lay up to 1500 eggs in a day when the conditions are ideal. They also produce scents that help the colony identify each other and regulate unity.

During every hive inspection, you have to check on the queen and see how she's doing. The queen must always be in good health to assure the health of the rest of the colony. The queen will be dependent on the other bees to tend to her every need. She is not even capable of feeding or grooming herself, so she'll always have some bees looking out for her.

The queen has a stinger but rarely stings. She'll only sting when threatened by another queen bee. Due to the important role the queen plays; you'll need to replace her with a younger stronger queen every new season. This will ensure you'll always have a strong colony with maximum productivity.

The worker bee

The worker bees form a large part of the colony. These are female like the queen but much smaller. Another differentiating feature is that they have pollen baskets in their hind legs which they use to ferry pollen with from the fields. The worker bee is very industrious always working in the hive and in the fields. Due to her very industrious nature, the worker bee has a much shorter lifespan. She only lives for 6 weeks in the active season.

At the early stages of her life, the worker bee will have some duties inside the hive such as taking care of the queen, looking after the younger bees and also removing any dead and diseased bees from the hive. They also take pollen collected by the field bees and place them in the right cells inside the hive. They also serve as guard bees protecting the hive against any threat. They check every returning bee to confirm they are part of the colony by scent. These can be referred to as the housekeeping duties and every worker bee has to take part in them. She'll then venture out of the hive to forage for nectar in the fields. After this stint she'll has become older and will return to the hive to take on some other responsibilities such as fanning the hive to control the humidity and temperatures inside.

The Drone Bee

The drone bee is bigger than the worker bee but smaller than the queen. They have a stout appearance. They are the only make bee in the colony. They are just a few hundreds of these bees at any one time. This is because their functions are limited and in fact are a liability to the hive at most of the time.

Their only role is procreation. They hang around the hive in case there is a new queen who will need to mate. The queen will only need to mate once. The mating occurs outside the hive around 300 feet in the air the queen will mate with several drones and all these will die immediately after mating. Just like the worker bee dies after stinging. This is because part of their anatomy explodes after the act. After mating, the worker bees will tolerate a few drones in the hive but once the winter season start kicking in, all drone will be kicked out of the hive. They eat much more food and are a threat to the survival of the other bees.

Chapter 6: Choosing a Bee Breed for your Hive

There are different races and strains of bees to choose from. We'll look at the most common races and their advantages as well as their disadvantages. In choosing the ideal breed, you'll also need to consider your location. Most of the honey bees in North America have been introduced from Europe, the Middle East and from Africa. There have been hybrid breeds developed over the years to suit the different climatic conditions. To determine the best breed, take a look at all of them and check on their pros and cons then make an informed decision.

Italian Bee

This is the most common bee race in North America. The Italian bee has a light yellowish hue with stripes of black and brown on the abdomen. The Italian breed broods early in the spring and continues till fall. This ensures a very large colony which is capable of collecting a lot of nectar thus more honey. However, the large colony will also require large reserves for honey for the winter period. Italian bees are very gentle. They are not defensive therefor a good option for a backyard hive. Their hue also makes them very attractive. They are resistant to many diseases. They will produce good amounts of honey in a season. They are good comb builders and good house cleaners hence the reduced risk of the colony getting diseased. They rarely swarm. The queen is easy to identify as other than being bigger than the other bees, she has the lightest color in the colony. This is a good bee for a beginner.

On the downside, the Italian bees are known for their robbing tendencies. They are more likely to attack a weaker colony and rob honey. This poses the risk of contracting a disease if the other colony is infected. Due to their large numbers, they can consume a lot of honey in the winter months. They are also prone to drifting to other colonies due to poor flight orientation.

The German Bee

The German bee is one of the oldest species of bees. It was introduced by German settlers to many parts of the world. It's dark in color and often called the dark bee. However, this breed is not the easiest to manage. It's highly defensive and prone to diseases. On other hand, the German bee is a hardy strain able to survive long cold winters. It was commonly found among wild bees but diseases have almost wiped it out.

The Carniolan Bee

This is another popular bee in North America. It is dark colored, greyish brown with stripes around the abdomen. It's originally from Eastern Europe.

The Carniolan bee colony is very active right from early spring. The colony builds up rapidly taking advantage of the early spring bloom to establish the colony. They are very docile and you won't need clothing and smoke when working with them. They are less likely to rob other colonies thus reduced chance of disease transmission. They are known of their wax combs and many bee keepers actually keep them for this reason besides the honey. They have a better flight orientation than the Italians hence they won't mix up with other colonies. They self-adjust their population depending on the available nectar. They are resistant to diseases and have a longer lifespan in comparison with other bees. This breed can survive long winters since they can keep a low population of worker bees then quickly build up during spring.

On the downside, these bees are more likely to swarm than other breeds due to the rapid buildup. Swarming is their natural way to decongest. This can lead to loss of a colony. You'll require being very vigilant to prevent swarming. They have trouble thriving in hot summers.

The Russian Bee

This is a very new stock of bee in the United States. It's native to Russia and has just been recently introduced to the United States due to its ability to survive the deadly varroa and tracheal mites which kill other colonies. The Russian bee broods only during the pollen flows and are good housekeepers. They do not rob and in general it's not good for this strain to mix with other colonies. Interbreeding greatly reduces their resistance to mites. It's a good honey producer.

On the con side, the Russian bee is more aggressive than the Italians and the Carniolan bee. Thus a first time bee keeper might encounter a few challenges when dealing with them. They are also more likely to swarm and only brood when there is enough forage. They are limited in the market being a recent breed to North America. However, you can easily purchase a queen.

There are other strains of bees which can be called commercial hybrid bees. These are bees that have been cross bred over the years to produce prolific bees with several desired qualities such as gentleness, winteriness, disease resistance and productivity. Such breeds are Midnite, Buckfast and Starline. Breeders are always looking to improve breeds. The secret to maintaining a healthy, vibrant, productive colony is by re queening each year. Go for a different queen breed each year to increase the vigor in your colony.

Before you select a breed over another especially being a beginner, seek as much information as possible from local beekeepers as regards the performance of the various breeds in terms of productivity, gentleness, disease resistance and winter survival. These are the 4 most important aspects you should look out for. Your location will heavily influence your choice. If you live in an area where winter falls hard and long, choose a breed that survives well in winter. If you live in a location where mites are common, you might try the Russian bee.

Chapter 7: Obtaining Your Initial Bee Colony

You have identified the bees you want, and now you have to get the actual bees. How do they get into your hive? You have some options to explore when you get to this point. You could purchase bees by mail, buy a small nucleus bee colony from a beekeeper, purchase a whole established colony or decide to catch swarming bees. All these are varied option to start you off. Let's look at them in more details.

CC0 Public Domain pixabay.com

Package bees

This is the most popular method among many beginner beekeepers. Ordering bees by mail might sound weird, but it's actually used and is very convenient. Most reputable bee breeders will package the bees and ship them to you.

The standard package will weigh around 3 pounds and will contain 11000-12000 bees. The size of the package will be similar to the large shoe packaging. The queen will be in a small screened cage inside the packaging secluded from the other bees. Tin containing sugar syrup will also be present which will provide food for the bee when they are in transit. One package is meant for a single hive hence the one queen. Order for all the hives you have.

Before making the order, you will need to ensure that your hive is ready to receive the new dwellers. Make arrangements with your chosen breeder who will confirm the shipping dates and estimate date of arrival. It will also be good to inform your local [post office about your expected package since they will not deliver bees to your home. they will call you to pick them at the post office. Make the post office people know that the special package needs to be kept in a cool, calm, dry place preferably dark.

Immediately the bees arrive, the post office will let you know since they do not want such kind of visitors at their place. Go to the post office and inspect the package carefully. Make sure that you actually see and hear the bees. It's normal to find some dead bees at the bottom of the package but not in alarming numbers. If you notice large number of these dead bees, fill put a claim form and inform your breeder. They will replace your bees.

When you get home, do not straight away take the bees to the hive, they will be tired and thirsty. Take the package in a cool dark place and spray them with cool water. You could use a spray bottle. You can also spray them with non-medicated sugar syrup. Now the bees are ready to go to the hive, take them there, this should be preferably at night. Have a feeder in the hive for their food as they won't find nectar right away.

Buying a nucleus bee colony

This is yet another good option. You could buy a nucleus bee colony from an established bee keeper. This is very practicable for those people living in areas where there are many bee farmers. A nuc will have 5 frames of brood and bees. An active young queen will also be present. This will be enough to start you off. These frames will come inside a box. You will then need to transfer the frames from the box to your hive. It's as simple as that. Actually this is simpler and more practical to a first time bee keeper than the mail package option. It is also less stressful on the bees since they are in the normal structure and won't travel long distances. You'll also be sure that the bees are used to the geographical location and the climate. They are going to find fields easier than completely new bees. Your local supplier will also be your source of advice on anything regarding the bees before you can fully understand them.

Buying an already established colony

This is another option. Some bee keepers sell an entire colony of bees together with the hive. However, this is not the best option for a beginner since an established colony is more difficult to manage. The colony will also be more aggressive and the large number of bees will make inspections a hard task. The colony will also be prone to swarming immediately after the change in location due the disturbance. The cost of the bee colony and the hive might also be on the higher side. If you are ready for it, then you could go ahead and find a farmer willing to sell.

CC0 Public Domain pixabay.com

Capturing a wild swarm

This is another even more challenging option. Getting a wild swarm and making it your own. It sounds interesting and really it is for an experienced bee keeper who wants to learn even more about bees. With the wild swarm, you don't choose the breed rather you take what gets to you. There is a risk of getting aggressive bees especially the Africanized bee which is known to be overly aggressive. If you choose this option, you can inform emergency services that you are interested in these bees. When they are called in to a place where a swarm has been found they'll inform you and let you keep the bees.

Chapter 8: How to Open Your Bee Hive

You have identified the breed of bees you want and have even gone ahead and put them in the hive. You'll need to monitor the bees closely during the first few days and regularly thereafter. You do not just approach the hive anyhow.

You always approach the hive from the rear or from the side. You don't want to collide with the bees getting out of the hive and those coming in. Doing so might anger them. Take time as you approach the hive to notice the pattern in which they dart around the hive. The aim is to avoid interfering with their flight path.

I am assuming you already have your protective clothing on and you have smoker in hand. These are not absolutely necessary, but at first, it's good to have them. Later when you get used to your bees and you understand their behavior, you might not need them. However always remain safe and do not expose any danger to yourself or others.

Blow some smoke at the entrance of the hive. Just a few puffs are enough. Do not overdo it to avoid injuring the bees. The smoke is meant to mask the scent the guard bees emit indicating intrusion to the hive. Open the top from one side and bellow some smoke inside as well. Allow a minute here too for the smoke to reach the bottom of the hive. You can now remove the top. Always remain gentle when working around bees. Do not make any sudden noises. The hive feeder will be found after the outer cover. If you are feeding the bees, you can go straight ahead and do so. If you are doing some inspection, remove the feeder as well. You will need the hive tool as its likely some parts will have stuck together. Loosen up any stuck part gently. If you need to hold something and there are bees around it, use your smoker to distract them and move them. You could also wipe them gently with a bee brush. Be careful not to kill or crush any bee.

Do not be afraid when handling bees, they are not interested in stinging you, they just want to mind their own business. In fact if they sting you they die. You just have to be calm, slow, careful and respectful. Concentrate fully on the task at hand and aim to learn as much as you can about the behavior of the bees.

You will remove the frames one by one looking at the brood pattern, any sign of disease and if the queen seems healthy. At first this will not be obvious to, you may need the direction of an experienced bee farmer. When pulling the frame, use your hive tool to pry the frame sideways, and then pull it all the way up. Do not twist the frame as you might kills any bees caught between the frames or even your queen. Crushing bees is a sure way to irritate them.

Chapter 9: Major Bee Diseases

Just like any other animals, bees too have some diseases which affect them. It's important as a beekeeper to be able to identify the diseases and thus take the required action in good time. It's so painful losing your bees to something you could have prevented. It's possible to lose an entire colony. Some diseases will be more common in some breeds than in others. Every time you carry out an inspection on your hive, be careful to note anything unusual. Some might be false alarms especially to inexperienced farmers but you better be safe than sorry. Let's look at the common diseases and how to look out for them

The American Foulbrood

This is a bacterial disease which affects the larvae and pupae. It's very devastating and can wipe out the entire brood. The infected larvae will change from their usual pearly white color to dark brown. They will soon die after they're capped. The brood pattern will not be compact but spotty and random. The capping of the dead larvae will sink inward and have tiny holes. There will be a foul smell emitting from the brood. If you find any of these signs, contact your local bee inspector for further diagnosis and treatment.

The European Foulbrood

The European foulbrood is a disease of the larvae. Here the larvae will die before they are capped unlike the American Foulbrood. Some of the signs to look out for include; spotty brood pattern, the infected larvae will be twisted in the bottom of the cell. They will be brown or light tan in color. Normal larvae are pearly white of glistering bright white. The larvae will die before being capped and thus you will be able to see them. Just like the AFB, there will be presence of a foul smell.

Nosema disease

This is dysentery of the bees. It's a disease that affects the intestinal tracts of the adult bees. Symptoms to look out for include; slow buildup up of colonies in the spring or no build up at all. Weak bees crawling aimlessly around the hive they may be shivering, spotting around the hive, this is streaks of feces appearing on the hive.

Chalk brood disease

This is a fungal infection that affects the bee larvae. You'll notice that most of these diseases affect the larvae. This is the most vulnerable part of the colony. However, the chalk brood disease is not as serious as the others. In most of the cases, the colony will overcome it by itself. No medication will be required. It is caused by damp condition usually in early spring. The infected larvae will become hard and may turn to chalky white color hence the name.

Sac brood disease

This is a viral disease that can be equated to the common cold in humans. Just like the chalk brood, it isn't much of a threat to the existence of the colony but may stress it out. Just like we humans are able to go through the common cold, the bees will also do it with sac brood. The larvae infected will turn yellow and dark brown. They appear in a water filled sac hence the name. There is no medication for sac brood and normally, the colony with survive it.

Colony collapse disorder

This is not technically a disease but is the most serious threat to the survival of bees in the world today. You've probably heard that bee colonies are reducing at an alarming rate all over the world; I talked briefly about this in the first chapter when we were looking at the reason why you should keep bees. Colony collapse disorder is responsible for this. The problem is so serious that there is a genuine concern of reduced agricultural output due to this. Bees are chiefly responsible for pollination and hence fertilization of plants.

Colony collapse disorder is the sudden disappearance of adult honey bees in the hive. You wake up one day and find you have no bees in your hive. The queen and a few young bees may be left but not enough to sustain the colony. In some cases, there are no bees left, even the queen has left. Honey and pollen will be present in the hive. What makes this condition mysterious is that bees do not leave a hive if they are rearing a brood. There is no explanation of the cause of the colony collapse disorder nor are there any proven ways to prevent it.

However, we can try to do a small part in keeping our bees healthy and happy and hopefully, they won't disappear mysteriously.

First you have to practice healthy bee management practices. This means that you'll be close to your bees, tending to their needs, checking out their wellbeing and understand their behavior. With this, you are likely to notice any slight changes and make appropriate interventions.

CC0 Public Domain pixabay.com

Anything that causes stress in your bees might be a contributory factor to colony collapse disorder. This may be an infection, lack of pollen, pests, inadequate ventilation, robbing from other colonies and many more. Always check out any stressful factor and address it well in advance. In the case of infections, use the right medication and if not sure, contact the state bee inspector to provide a prescription.

Replace frames every two years to reduce the chances of residual chemicals being present in the old wax. Modern chemicals might be cause of the sudden collapse of the colony, though this is just a speculation. When controlling mites and pests, use integrated pest management option to reduce the instances when you need to use chemicals in your hive.

Lastly you could decide to make your voice heard on this issue. As a bee keeper, this is a serious threat to your precious hobby and if nothing is done, we might have no bees in years to come. Funding for bee research should be increased. Encourage more people to keep bees as this will lead to more awareness too.

Chapter 10: When to Harvest Honey from Your Hive

You have identified the breed of bees you want and have even gone ahead and put them in the hive. You'll need to monitor the bees closely during the first few days and regularly thereafter. You do not just approach the hive anyhow.

There is no defined time when you should harvest your honey. Normally you harvest your honey when the beehive is filled with cured and capped honey. This is usually at the end of a nectar flow season.

CC0 Public Domain pixabay.com

For a first time bee keeper, you'll be lucky to have some honey in late summer. Your new colony hasn't built a large enough population to produce enough honey. They will need a full season to do so. The little honey they produce will be just enough for them. You should always keep in mind that bees produce honey as food storage for the winter and when the nectar flow is minimal. You should only take the surplus honey from them.

You will know you can harvest the honey when a frame contains more than 80 percent of capped honey. You could also choose to wait till the bees have filled all the frames with capped honey and have a bountiful harvest. Honey stored in open cells that is not capped is usually not ready for harvesting. You can however carry out a quick test to find out if it is cured. Remove the frame and gently shake it, if you find honey flowing then this is not cured and not ready for harvesting. It cannot even be referred to as honey but rather nectar. If you harvest this stuff, it's likely to ferment and get spoilt. Pure honey doesn't ferment and never goes bad.

You should harvest honey only before the cold season or after the cold season preferably in spring. During winter and any other cold time, the honey will thicken in the com or even granulate making it impossible to remove it from the comb. It's easiest to harvest honey in late summer.

You will need necessary honey harvesting equipment depending on the type of honey you want to harvest.

Extracted honey

Extracted honey is the most common type of honey. This is the honey extracted from the combs and packaged in containers for selling inn stores. For this type of honey, you will need an uncapping knife, an extractor and a sieve to strain the honey. You will slice off the honey comb using the uncapping knife then extract the honey using the extractor (also called a spinner) you should then strain the honey using a sieve to get out the occasional bee and wax in the honey. You can now package the honey in containers ready for consumption. The extractor can be expensive to purchase and it would be much cheaper to hire one if you are not a big time bee keeper.

Comb honey

This is honey still in the combs as the bees packaged it. There is a huge market for comb honey as well. This type of honey is best produced after a strong nectar flow. Harvesting this type of honey is very easy as you just need to get the entire honey comb and package it. Its eaten whole both the wax and the honey.

Regardless of how you plan to harvest your honey, you will have to remove bees from the honey supers even before you can extract the honey.at this time, bees will be very protective of the honey. You will need to be adequately clothed and have your smoker in hand. When you extract the frames from the honey supers, smoke the bees lightly or use a bee brush to wipe them off. You could also try to shake the frame at the entrance of the hive though this might be challenging with the deep frames instance they will be heavy. If you have somebody helping you, this should be possible. After you have cleared the bees of the frames, place them in an empty super or a bucket and make sure you cover with a board or towel, otherwise bees will come back and start eating the honey.

CC0 Public Domain pixabay.com

Conclusion

Backyard beekeeping is an interesting and rewarding pastime. You'll get to learn so much about bees more than you could ever imagine. There's also the feeling that you are doing something worthwhile for the environment which is a great feeling. There has been an increase in the interest in backyard beekeeping in the recent times. This is great news since nature needs these bees. Bees are great creatures that deserve to remain with us due to the very important role they play. Anything that threatens their existence threatens us too.

It would be good to find a beekeeping society or community near you and join them. They will be glad that you have developed an interest in beekeeping and help you along the journey. You will get lots of advice as you can as well share your experiences with people who share this interest with you. The community will also be a good place to check for where to hire some equipment you might not have such as the extractor. You can search online or at the local state bee inspector office for contacts.

You may also enjoy:

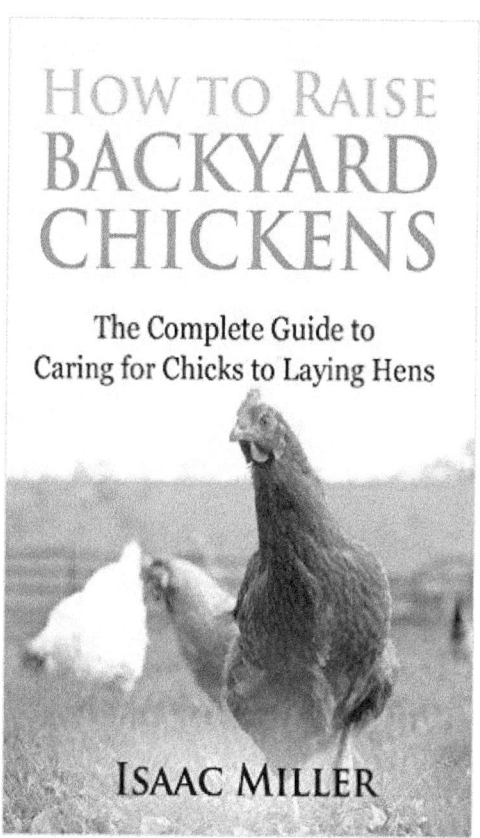

www.ingramcontent.com/pod-product-compliance
Lightning Source LLC
Chambersburg PA
CBHW072020290526
45787CB00013B/1519